ASSERTIVE BEHAVIOUR
&
DELEGATION

Phil Sinclair

The entire copyright of this publication including all intellectual rights are the property of the publisher. The book is sold subject to the condition that it shall not in full, or in part, by way of trade, or otherwise, be resold, hired out, copied or stored in an electronic retrieval system other than that of the purchaser, or circulated in any form without the publisher's consent.

COPYRIGHT

Phil Sinclair t/a Leader's-Edge (RSA) who are the publishers and copyright holders of this publication.

Phil Sinclair (Author) is well-known for his contribution to the publishing of training and self-development materials for young managers in his home country of South Africa. His audio seminars have been studied by more than 100,000 executives world-wide. He has received several prestigious international awards for his work in small business promotion. He is author of several books on Human Resources subjects and twelve internationally used management training programmes.

Phil is currently publications director for Leader's-Edge (RSA) a business which has since 1984 specialised in publishing and distributing self-development materials for managers and aspiring leaders.

INTRODUCTION

Straightway let's look at the benefits to you of reading and learning from this book.

Assertive Behaviour and Delegation are both skills of managing personal and interpersonal relationships within your daily role as a manager. By acquiring the skill of being "assertive" and also knowing how to "delegate" you can expect several real benefits. First you will be better able to deal with every situation that requires personal interaction. You will get more achievement out of your day and can expect more recognition for your achievements.

Second, you will find that you are better liked and better understood as a business manager, which is a big part of becoming a business leader.

Thirdly, another important part of becoming a business leader, is an ability to get more done, more effectively *through* those people who work with you, under you, and even above you.

And fourth, with what you will be learning here you

will experience a significant rise in your own self-esteem.

You will learn to like yourself because you will have become more adept at personal interactions. You will be creating the right mental attitude and you will be doing the right things to cultivate a motivated following.

CONTENTS

Part One ASSERTIVE BEHAVIOUR

Understanding Assertive Behaviour
The Assertive Management Style
Transactional Analysis
The Foundation of Human Behaviour
Self-examination
Maintaining a positive and assertive attitude
Games People Play
Planning the Confrontation
17-point Assertiveness Checklist
Conclusion

Part Two DELEGATION

Introduction
Reasons for Delegating
The Concept of Delegation
Interpersonal Relationships
The Work Assignment
Barriers to Effective Delegation
Effective Delegation
Conclusion

Part One

ASSERTIVE BEHAVIOUR

Assertiveness Behaviour is a skill that helps you move up from "management", which often pushes unmotivated half-productive people from behind, to "Leadership" where <u>you</u> are at the head of a team of motivated, dedicated and productive followers.

The kind of words we hear in management today are, motivation, shared-vision, participation, mutual trust, employee involvement and teamwork.
These words seem to indicate a modern management style which is "softer" than the authoritarian style of yester-year where we heard words like; obedience, order, control and hierarchy.

But modern management isn't "softer", the contrast is that it's much more people oriented and democratic in style. This didn't come about because we've evolved naturally into caring sharing managers, it came about because this style of management and leadership has been proven to produce the best results in terms of productivity and profitability.

But democratic management brings with it a whole new set of demands on the manager, who can no longer sit in his ivory tower, passing down written orders and never meeting with anyone in particular on a personal level.

He, or she, must now continually meet face-to-face with employees, subordinates, peers and upper management. You must learn the skill of personal interaction to the extent that "motivation" and "shared-vision" become essential by-products of every such meeting. In short, you have to understand something of human behaviour, of different personality types and how to recognise them and how to deal with them.
You need to know how to influence changes in human behaviour in order to achieve your goals and those of your business... all of which needs to be done <u>assertively</u>.

So let's begin by examining what assertiveness is, in the management context and what it isn't.

Imagine that one of your workers, Peter Briggs, has been late for work three times in the last month. The first two times you decided to say nothing about it because Peter Brigg's attendance record has been pretty good till now. But you've been boiling up about it because he has a responsible position and he holds up the production line every time he's late. You can't afford for him to develop a pattern of being habitually late, so you haul him into your office. And the conversation goes something like this...

"Peter, this is now the <u>third</u> time you've pitched up late. I've said nothing about it before...in fact i've given you two chances. But you're just taking advantage of my good nature. You're in the hot seat now and i'm going to be watching your attendance record closely, so you'd better shape up and stop letting us down like this...that is if you want to continue working here!"

The speaker leans forward as he dresses Peter Briggs down. He raises his voice for emphasis and he points an accusative finger as he delivers the words ....

"You're in the hot seat now!"

What has actually happened here?

The boss has let fly with his bottled up emotion. He has passed a <u>judgment</u>...and a sentence on Peter Briggs. He has attempted to get his own way by shaping up Peter Briggs and has done it by breathing fire and brimstone over the latecomer.

He has used <u>aggressive</u> tactics to try to get his own way. He believes that he has the right to expect punctuality and he has demanded that right.

In doing this a situation is created where the boss-character may win over the character of Peter Briggs. But Peter Briggs will harbour resentment over the way in which he's been treated.
He'll be thinking: *"Where does this guy get off? I've given him years of good service and just because I'm late a couple of times he treats me like a dog. I'll show him who's the dog around here".*

Peter Briggs will definitely feel that the power-wielding boss has won and that he has "lost".
And this is what we call an "I win-you lose" sort of situation. The boss may have been well intentioned but he didn't create the solution to the problem that would produce the greatest dividends. In fact he didn't even find out what Peter Briggs problem really was as being late might well be just a symptom of some far greater problem. Peter Briggs feels confident that the boss won't really fire him. He would probably tow the line for a week, or two, then come in late again. But this time he'd plan a really good excuse in advance.

There are other outcomes to situations.
They are... the "I lose -you win" situation, where the other person walks off having gained something, leaving you to mop up after them...and the "I lose-you lose" situation, where nobody is really satisfied with the outcome.

Here's an "I lose-you win" outcome using the same example. Peter Briggs is again called into the manager's office...
"Peter this is the third time you've been late recently. We expect our senior staff to set a good example, so I'm going to warn you about it just this once!"

...and Peter Briggs replies that he's sorry but the public transport service hasn't been performing to schedule, there isn't anything he can do about that, as his car is old and he can't trust it to drive into the office any more.
However, if the boss could review his salary he could afford a new car and there would no longer be a problem of lateness. Failing that the time table should be sorted out soon. The boss replies

"For your sake Peter, I hope that it is!"

Peter Briggs has clearly won, not only the

confrontation, but he has somehow managed to reserve himself the right to come late on further occasions. The boss has lost because he feels that the problem has not been solved. The boss is frustrated and annoyed with himself as well as Peter Briggs.

"For your sake Peter, I hope that it is!"

Now here's an "I lose - you lose" situation using the same example. The boss calls Peter Briggs down and says to him.

"Peter you're going to have to shape up. I can't tolerate this lateness of yours. One more time and you're out."

And Peter Briggs replies that he thinks he has good reasons for being late. If the boss wants to fire him he'll give those reasons to his union and land the boss with a whole heap of problems. The boss replies...

"Get out of my office and get back to work.. I don't intend to be threatened by the likes of you!"

Now both the boss and Peter Briggs feel frustrated and annoyed with each other. They have both "lost" in the confrontation, which has resulted in a stalemate.

The "I win - you lose" situation, the "You win - I lose" situation and the "You lose - I lose" situation all have, in some way a <u>negative</u> outcome because each time somebody has to be a loser and what do we know about losers? They are sore. They are unhappy and they may harbour grudges. They are tense, annoyed, frustrated, uncomfortable and far less likely to be motivated than happy people. Motivation comes primarily out of a sense of well-being and "well-being" is developed out of winning situations, not losing situations.

THE DESIRED OUTCOME

So what are we looking for? What is the <u>desired</u> outcome from any kind of personal interaction, or confrontation?

The ideal situation is the "I win - you win" situation. This is at the centre of all assertiveness training. Both parties go away contented, or at least in agreement, with the outcome. This is the only desirable outcome to a personal interaction in the workplace. The "I win- you win" situation is arrived at by "human-engineering" the situation using assertiveness techniques.

The Aggressive Management Style
Assertiveness is often associated with aggressiveness and authority. People who believe that they are under-assertive believe that they should become more aggressive speakers, that they should summon up more courage to wield the authority afforded them by their job titles. Tell subordinates what for..stand up to the boss a bit more., you know the kind of thing. But that <u>isn't</u> assertiveness ...that's <u>aggressiveness</u> and aggressiveness won't give you the desired result of personal satisfaction and getting the job done better through more effective use of your people. Here's why...

Nobody likes aggressive people. If you think that perhaps you should become more aggressive, consider...do <u>you</u> like aggressive people?

Do you mix easily in their company? Would you willingly share your lunch, or coffee break, with an aggressive person?

There's a popular misconception that you have to be aggressive to succeed in business. Well, that just isn't so. Aggressive behaviour invokes aggressive reactions and often results in inter-personal conflict.. Aggressive people tend to have few friends around the office. They may bludgeon short-term co-operation out of those who allow themselves to be intimidated but in the long term that compliance, or co-operation that is essential for your development as a leader, will be lacking.

So aggressive people are not generally liked and as everyone on earth has a deep-down desire to be liked, aggressive people become unhappy in themselves and stressed up.

The Passive Management Style
At the other end of the scale you have the manager who is very <u>passive</u> in their management style. He, or she, wants to be everyone's f riend.   They don't want to step on any toes... they want to be liked and respected and feel that giving way quite a bit is a good way to get the staff feeling good about them. This kind of manager wants to help people out all the time. Often says..."Here, I know that's a tough assignment, let me do it for you!"

 In a confrontational situation, this type of manager often ends up the "loser" and goes around berating himself, or herself, when they've tried so hard to be understanding and helpful to everyone around them.

They don't have the success formula and they know it.

So on the one hand you have the aggressive management style characterised by a need to win at other people's expense. If necessary by treading on people, putting people down, humiliating them and violating their rights as human beings. This aggressive behaviour can also be called <u>over-assertiveness</u>.

On the other hand you have very passive behaviour which is characterised by failure to stand up for reasonable rights, giving in too easily to other people's opinions, and being swayed where important decisions are concerned. This type of behaviour can be called <u>under assertive</u> behaviour. Aggressive, or over-assertive behaviour takes the <u>fight</u> path. Passive, or under-assertive behaviour takes the <u>flight</u> path. And neither of these paths really lead you to your personal or business success goals.

The reason for this is that both the aggressive, or over-assertive and the passive, or under-assertive, styles of management stop you from arriving at that all important "I win - you win" situation. So there has to be another choice that does allow you to turn all personal interactions into "win-win" situations, where both parties feel that their rights as human beings are being upheld.

The Assertive Management Style
The third choice is called "the assertive management style". It is characterised by a manager standing up for his, or her, own rights in such a way as not to violate the basic rights of the other person, or people involved. Whilst not violating the basic rights of others involved, the assertive management style does allow you to express your feelings, opinions, or needs in a direct, honest and <u>appropriate</u> manner. The assertive management style is calculated to produce the "I win - you win" situation.

It probably occurs to you at this stage that the assertive management style is nothing more than steering a course down the middle. Just be sure not to be too aggressive, or too passive and you're there! You're being assertive! This isn't a bad observation, or a bad place to start. But there's a lot more to the assertive style of management than just holding your temper down on the one side and standing up and speaking out on the other.

Assertiveness sets out to achieve personal happiness

for you in your job, your success as an individual, and your success in getting things done through your people. But how do these things happen? What's the one thing that governs these happenings?

The one thing that will give you success results is YOUR ABILITY TO INFLUENCE AND CHANGE HUMAN BEHAVIOUR...your ability to influence and change human behaviour. If people are not doing what you want them to do for you, or they are doing things that cause you concern, or have some other negative impact on you, such as worry, embarrassment, loss of esteem, loss of time, loss of freedom, unhappiness...then a "people problem" exists and you must have a way of INFLUENCING THOSE PEOPLE CONCERNED TO CHANGE THEIR BEHAVIOUR, that is if the problem can be genuinely laid at the door of someone else.

If the problem should be truthfully laid at your own door, then what is required is <u>a change of your own behaviour</u>.

YOU CAN'T CHANGE PEOPLE!

An important point to note is that you cannot change

someone's personality, not even your own, but you can definitely, by using the right techniques, influence a switch in BEHAVIOUR. If someone in your office talks too much and gets too little done in a day, you can't change the personality of a friendly person who simply likes talking. But you can influence that person to change their behavior at the office...and you can do it without becoming aggressive, without having that person feel that any basic human rights have been violated and without losing that all-important "I Win – You Win" situation.

THE FOUNDATION OF HUMAN BEHAVIOUR

If you're going to learn how to influence human behaviour you must first understand something of the "foundation of human behaviour". What makes people behave the way they do? Why do *you* respond in the way that you do?

 To find out, we look into a study of human behaviour that has been used with great success for many years. Originally it was developed by psychiatrists as an aid to analyzing their patients ...and it still is used extensively by the medical profession because it helps doctors to understand behavioral problems of their clients. More recently behavioral scientists saw that it had great value in helping business managers to understand the behaviour of those who worked around them. I'm referring to what is now commonly known as "Transactional Analysis", or TA.

TRANSACTIONAL ANALYSIS

In Transactional Analysis it is supposed that all personalities are made up of a combination of three "ego states". They are:

1. The Child Ego"
2. The "Parent Ego"
3. The "Adult Ego"

The Child Ego state is where creativity comes from and from where emotions are felt. It's the area where feelings of warmth come from..feelings of completeness and satisfaction. But also feelings of frustration, anger and annoyance.

Before you were old enough to use judgment, logical, rational and analytical problem solving, you just used your feelings. The child ego state is your emotional centre. It lets you react with tears, with laughter, with jealousy. It's the area where you feel liked...or want to be liked. You want to be touched, loved, helped, soothed.

You may also want to get attention in other ways through your Child Ego State. It's easy to imagine a child lying on the floor, kicking and thumping in rage, in order to let its annoyance be felt. Children do that kind of thing but do grown-ups? Yes they do!

Whenever you see someone thump their desk, scream break and shout and throw an office tantrum, something, go red in the face, burst into tears, silently sulk, plot revenge ...or when you see someone who is sad and needs cheering, who is lacking confidence and needs encouragement, who is bursting with laughter, or playing or telling a joke, that's the Child Ego State that you are observing.

Physically the Child Ego State may be characterised in the way a person might dress. Bright clothes, a badge in the lapel, eccentricities in Jewelry, all indicate Child Ego. Often it can also be observed in the car that a person chooses to drive and in a person's behaviour whilst watching his, or her favourite sport.

But I want to add that there is absolutely nothing wrong with having a strong child ego. I think that

Picasso probably had a strong child ego. Many creative geniuses, sportsmen and women and fun-loving people from all walks of life have a developed child ego.

They are very emotional people, people who feel a lot, who like a lot of attention and who usually express themselves vibrantly. It would be more wrong for a person to have no Child Ego, or a severely restrained Child Ego State. This would indicate suppressed emotion, or at least a deadly dull personality. The Child Ego state can be a very strong positive force within a person but also, note this....

Sometimes the Child Ego in a person uses negative attention-getters when positive ones aren't available.

For example a person might be turning up late for work because this is their way of attracting the attention that they need.

He, or she, may be bringing domestic problems to work, to get other people to feel sorry for them. A person might develop a headache, or commit some unacceptable form of behaviour in the office, just to get noticed. So behaviour from the child ego might be positive and it might be negative. But the Child Ego state, whether positive, or negative at the time, is to a greater or lesser extent in all of us, as are the other two Ego States.

The Parent Ego state is the second part of our personality. If the Child Ego is the "feeling" part of the personality, the Parent Ego is the " judgmental" part.

It's the part that holds all of those beliefs that your parents gave you. The knowledge of what is good and what is bad, right, or wrong, is all packed away in your parent ego. In the parent state we behave something like our parents did before us. Hear somebody say "*Do that one more time and I'll have your guts for garters*" and what ego state are they coming from? The Parent State! When we make judgments based on our own beliefs, it's the parent ego talking. For example...

"People don't like coloured tiles in the bathroom, do the whole thing in white please!"

It's also the Parent Ego talking when a person starts commanding and demanding. Physically the Parent Ego State might be recognised by such words as...

"As your boss I expect you to..".

"Come on now move it! We can't wait all day!"

"One more time like that and we'll dock your holiday pay, understand!"

" I thought I told you to do it <u>this</u> way!"

The Parent Ego state is easy to recognise because it is "judgmental" It's pretty obvious when somebody is saying something because they hold a preconceived notion like...*you're too old for this job...women do that kind of thing better than men...blondes are dumb..., children should be seen and not heard...subordinates should bend a bit at the knee.*

The Parent Ego is inflexible and it doesn't show any spontaneous feelings of happiness, or grief.
The Parent Ego is not creative, neither is it emotional. The authoritarian attitude, the sarcastic response, intolerance and shows of annoyance, these are all signs of the Parent Ego popping up during an interaction. As with the Child Ego state, like it or not, you do have a Parent Ego state as part of your personality. How much it comes to the fore, how you

deal with it in yourself and when you're faced with it from others, is all part of assertiveness training.

The Adult Ego.
The <u>third</u> ego state that concerns students of Transactional Analysis is the "Adult Ego". If the Child Ego state is the <u>feeling</u> part of our personality and the parent ego state is the <u>judgmental</u> part of our personality, then the "Adult Ego" state is the <u>thinking</u> part of our personality.

Our Adult Ego is responsible for processing information. It helps us with problem solving. It supplies us with logic. It is rational and analytical. This ego state is flexible and able to help us to make decisions. The adult ego, when in control and to the forefront, helps us to behave in an independent and adult manner. It does not permit outbursts of emotion, nor does it allow us to judge situations using past beliefs and preconceived notions drilled into us some time ago by our parents, or some other authority.

It is the Adult Ego which helps us to view things rationally in an adult manner.

Most important, the Adult Ego is what we can apply in a logical, rational and analytical manner to switch and control our own behaviour and the behaviour of others.

When we are aware of these three "Ego States", we can recognise when our behaviour is childlike...please note that I don't say "childish".

Or we can recognise that we are making judgments out of pre-conceived notions and behaving in a "parental" manner..not giving the other person an opportunity to disagree, for example.

We can use our Adult Ego State to come to grips with personal and interpersonal problems. Study yourself and study those people with whom you meet, and now that you're aware of the three ego states, you will see them constantly coming into play, shifting from, one ego state to another to suit the situation.

In fact it doesn't take much practice to slip from one ego state to another, once you are aware of the ego state from which you are behaving. If you are suddenly aware that you are conducting a one-sided argument, being intolerant of the other person, you can easily switch yourself into the adult mode, so becoming more rational and thoughtful about what the problem really is.

Similarly if someone is performing from his, or her, child ego, you know that you are dealing with an emotionally charged situation. There won't be any point in responding from your Parent Ego as thoughtfulness and rational discussion will be required. So you will deal with an emotionally charged person, not by showing annoyance and parental intolerance, but by using the open-mindedness and directness of your Adult Ego.

A little later we'll examine some actual examples of the three ego states in confrontational and problem-solving situations but for now, let's go back to "The Foundation For Human Behaviour". The more you know about the personality and type of behaviour that confronts you, the more easily you will be able to deal with and influence a switch of attitude.

I'M OK – YOU'RE O.K.

Have you heard the term "I'm OK - You're O.K"? It's an important part of the Foundation of human Behaviour - and vital information for you in practicing assertiveness.

In order to be assertive you have to first feel O.K.

about yourself. You have to believe in yourself, in your abilities, the way you do your job and also the way you run your personal life. You should be aware of your values, your self-worth. You should hold yourself in good esteem.

In <u>addition</u> you should also develop the feeling that the person with whom you're dealing is also "O.K." That person might not enthuse you, he, or she, might make plenty of mistakes, maybe not do things your way. But nonetheless, that person is O.K. You respect that person as a human being. Someone who has rights. Someone whom you are not going to use your power and position to step on, to crush, to steam-roller out of sight.

The theory is that if you treat a person as O.K., then they will be more likely to co-operate with you and treat <u>you</u> as O.K. in return. "I'm O.K. - You're O.K. is the ideal situation but in practice, it doesn't always work like that. It takes practice to engineer the situation.

What often happens is that the manager who is used to operating out of his Parent Ego state will have the idea that ""I'm OK – You're NOT OK". After all you are a subordinate and subordinates are NOT ok. They do not give you any compliance unless you give them a swift kick. I am sure you have met this type of person.

"What do you think that I pay you for...try using that thing that you call a brain! No wonder your work is messy - you're a really messy kind of person, just look at yourself!"

There it is the Parent Ego talking - the speaker feels O.K. but the person he's addressing is not allowed to feel at all O.K.

Then there's the type of person who feels.."You're O.K. - I'm not O.K".

He, or she, is often a shy person who is lacking in confidence and unwilling to make a commitment. Thinks that everybody else is more capable, better looking, has gone further in life. This kind of person often lacks self-expression and will do almost anything to avoid upsetting people, or causing any kind of conflict.

He, or she, is under-assertive and a loser in the "win-win" formula that we discussed earlier. There is a dangerous weakness in this kind of behaviour. The "I'm not O.K." type of person can be emotionally dishonest. They can say things that they don't really believe, or mean, to avoid conflict. They can act nice, without really being nice at all. Here's an example...

"Look I'll do what I can for you. I'll bring it up at the next board meeting"

Notice, there's no commitment... and it's probably an empty promise.

The "I'm not O.K" type is usually expressing themselves out of their child ego state. They were brought up to believe, from an early age, that other kids were stronger, more capable, more attractive, brighter.

So what do you do if you find that you are yourself behaving from the Child Ego State? You call upon some rational reasoning from your Adult ego state...you come to terms with yourself by rationalising that maybe you're not such a hard done by person.

What do you do if you have to interact with a person who feels themselves "not O.K."?

 You detect whether they are performing from their Child Ego state, which might be characterised by some emotion of fear, of sadness, of gladness, or of anger; or whether they are performing from their

Parent Ego which might be characterised by an unwillingness to budge on a certain issue, an unwillingness to listen to your arguments, plus a few physical indicators, such as a tense jaw thrust forward, tensed shoulders, clenched hands, tightly crossed legs, glaring, or staring.

You then attempt, through the patient use of logical, rational and analytical thinking to help the other person switch from their Child, or Parent Ego State into their Adult ego state.

The more the person who thinks that they are not O.K. can shift into his Adult Ego State, the more O.K. he, or she, will feel. And when both persons feel "O.K." the most co-operation will be obtained.

The final situation in this part of the Foundation for Human Behaviour is the person who feels "Not-O.K" himself but then he, or she, doesn't think that you are O.K. either! This person doesn't like himself, and he doesn't like anyone else either. He's the chip on-the-shoulder problematic type of person who feels that everyone is out to get him.
 Often he, or she will be a secret, or even open drinker. A very hard kind of person to work with. This kind of person is not often found in a managerial

position. He's usually the menial worker who is always heard moaning and grumbling under his breath.

Everything he does is under sufferance. With this type of person you have to work hard to produce an "I'm O.K.- You're O.K." situation.

You have to slowly build layers of trust and understanding. Use the rational and analytical thought process of your Adult Ego to slowly help him build respect for himself and then later for you. First, however, you might do well to consider that such a personality might be happier and more responsive working somewhere other than with you.

Do the talents that he brings to your work outweigh the time and trouble that you'll need to spend on making an "I'm O.K - You're O.K." feeling from him?

Leaders get the "Edge" by thinking creatively and acting assertively. Their thoughts and actions promote willing involvement and openness from motivated "followers".

SOME SELF EXAMINATION

It's time for a little self-examination. You can't train yourself to be correctly assertive without first knowing in which areas you need to improve, so I'm going to give you a list of ten questions to answer and ten statements to consider.

The ten questions are to do with your comfort when you have to communicate with others.
The ten statements are to do with how you see the importance of interaction with other people.

First the ten "comfort in communication" questions. Rate your answers either "no discomfort" "little discomfort", "uncomfortable" or "very uncomfortable".

1. How do you feel on those occasions when you have lost control of yourself?

2. How do you feel about disagreeing with people...clients, customers etc?

3. How do you feel about expressing your opinions during meetings?

4. How do you feel about making a bad impression?

5. How do you feel about disagreeing with people in a higher position than you?

6. How do you feel about having to introduce people to each other?

7. How do you feel about asking a favour from someone?

8. How do you feel about talking to people who might be better educated, or more qualified than you are?

9. How do you feel about dealing with "pushy" subordinates or customers?

10. How do you feel about having a lot of authority over other people?

You might like to stop the here and run back over the ten questions so you can consider your answers.

If your average score to the test is "very uncomfortable" then you are generally very under-assertive, even submissive, and probably you try to avoid personal communications.
Your feeling of "I'm O.K" has to be worked on with

positive affirmations. (I will deal with that a little later in the book).

If your average is "little discomfort" then you are generally assertive and responding appropriately to interpersonal communications. If your answer is an average of "no discomfort", then you are probably being over-assertive, even aggressive, and too insensitive to the feelings of others.

Here are the ten statements that test your beliefs about the importance of interpersonal communications.

Simply answer these questions "True" or "False".

1. If you really care for someone, they'll know it without you having to tell them.

2. Arguing makes people feel bad, and it doesn't change anyone's mind.

3. It's improper for a man to argue with a woman.

4. If you aren't 100% sure of your opinion, it's best to say nothing.

5. You should always try to fulfil a customer's

request, even if it's unreasonable.

6. If someone annoys you, for the sake of peace, it's best to keep quiet.

7. Contradicting a domineering person doesn't pay, since you will just make him angry.

8. By insisting on having your own way you will usually hurt someone's feelings.

9. You usually lose the arguments that you have. Other people seem to find it easy to win.

10. It's always best to check what other people think before doing anything.

If your answers are mainly under the rating of "True", you are very sensitive to personal communications, you are under-assertive and probably you suffer from stress as a result of this. At the other end of the scale an all "False" rating would put you at being over-assertive and even aggressively pushy. Somewhere in the middle would be the appropriately assertive response.

But why make the change ...don't we just accept what

we are and learn to live with it? Absolutely not! Assertive behaviour is the only appropriate behaviour for leaders.

If you are under-assertive and even submissive you might think that people in general will like you and accept you because you are so amenable and that you will lead an uncomplicated, undemanding and comfortable way of life where you won't get into trouble. In fact you will possibly be disliked because people will be continually frustrated in dealing with what they see as personal weaknesses. You will end up feeling unhappy in a management position and definitely "not O.K."

You might imagine it's good to be aggressive and the strongest, most powerful, beast in the herd. You will climb the career ladder fast by getting things done your way. You will bend people into compliance, get respect for your power and frighten people into submission and acceptance of your point of view. In fact you will create antagonism, people will NOT like, or trust you. You will encounter opposition from more aggressive people and a lot of your efforts will be sabotaged along the way.

The assertive manager develops and maintains

workable relationships with people. He, or she, is consistently open and attentive to the needs of others, whilst not being manipulated. The likely results of this behaviour style is that you will become an inspirational person with a team of motivated followers.

HOW TO DEAL WITH UNDER-ASSERTIVENESS

How do you deal with under-assertiveness? Make a mental shift from the Child Ego State which allows you to be emotional and fearful of confrontational situations.

This is what gives you that "very uncomfortable" feeling in the questions you've just answered.

Make a shift from the Parent Ego state which gave you those "beliefs" or pre-conceived notions that were responsible for the "true" rating in the last list of statements. Shift into your Adult Ego State and give your behaviour some rational and analytical thinking.

You can quell the Child and Parent Ego and slip into your Adult Ego State, just by telling yourself that you want to. There is also a practical way of making the shift from under-assertiveness to assertiveness by raising your self-esteem. Get yourself a pack of small blank cards and write down on them a number of self-talk statements. Nobody else ever has to see these cards so make the statements from the heart.

Here is a suggested list, one statement per card. By writing something similar, whatever applies to you personally, onto your cards, you will be effectively programming yourself for greater esteem each time that you read through the pack of cards.

I am a worthwhile person
People will pay the price that I set on myself I have values as a person
I have personal power. What I do matters.
My work is important work and I'm up to the responsibility.
It is important to my self-respect to turn down unreasonable
requests.
I have a right to expect courtesy and respect.
Not telling the truth about how I think and feel is selfish.
"Giving in" teaches others to mistreat me.
Not telling others how I react to them cheats them of a chance to change.
Sacrificing my rights can destroy a relationship.
Standing up for my rights shows that I respect myself.
When I do what I think is right, I feel better about me.

I have a right to express myself as long as I don't hurt others.

A set of self-talk cards like this definitely does help you to programme your subconscious mind for a more positive and assertive attitude.

If you're feeling less than 100% O.K. about yourself, just flick through the cards, in private, no-one else need ever know what is written on the cards.
It does work. And once it's worked for you, you will be able to help another person to reach his, or her "O.K." position by reinforcing his, or her, mental attitude with more positive thinking.

You can use the same sentences that you wrote on your talk cards only instead of "I" the message simply becomes "you". For example; "you are a worthwhile person". "We like having you around here". "You will be paid the price that you set on yourself". "Your good work will be rewarded". "You are valued as a person, Jim, sometimes I don't know what we'd do without you around here". "You can help people meet their needs". "Jim, I think that you have leadership qualities that you're not using". "You have personal power". "What you do matters". "Jim, you're in the driving seat and I see you pointed in a positive direction".

Instead of showing the cards to yourself to help you feel more "O.K.", you are using the same positive affirmations, logical rational words from your Adult Ego, to make someone else feel O.K., to feel relaxed in your company and more disposed towards shifting their attitude when you get around to making a request.

SUMMARY of EGO STATES

Let's recap a little on what's been covered. We talked about the "I win - You win" situation as being the most desirable situation for productive negotiation, or problem-solving where interpersonal exchanges are called for.

We then talked about "The Three Ego States", the Child Ego, the Parent Ego and the Adult Ego. When you know what you're dealing with you can deal with it better - words and behaviour from the other person indicate which of the three ego states is being used.

You respond by using your Adult Ego, which is rational thinking, direct and unemotional to help the other person switch into his, or her Adult Ego State. To do this you should strive for the "I'm O.K. - You're O.K." feeling between yourself and the other person.

If the "O.K." feeling isn't there for you personally ...if you feel oversensitive, frustrated, annoyed, angry, or even insensitive, blunt, irrational, then use your own adult ego to shift away from set beliefs and judgmental behaviour coming from your parent ego, and from emotional feelings that come from your child ego.

A practical way to do this is by programming yourself with self-talk written down on a series of privately held cards. If the "O.K." feeling isn't there for the person with whom you're interacting try to redirect the kind of message you'd use for yourself to build the "O.K." feeling of the other person. In being "assertive" at all times you show respect for the other person's rights and values, including their right to express their feelings, opinions and needs, whilst at the same time you give a response which is appropriate to the situation and which does not violate your own rights and needs.

The more knowledge you have of the person with whom you're dealing - the more able will you be to influence their behaviour. So I now want to tell you about some of the "games that people play" to intentionally, or unintentionally, get one over on you and make themselves feel more O.K. Here they are and how to recognize them. There are several.

.

THE GAMES PEOPLE PLAY

The Victim
One game is called "The Victim". This is the person who wants you to feel sorry for him, or her. They want you to take them under your wing and do things for them..ease their burden..lighten the heavy load that life has put upon them.

This person tries to attract your attention, or interest, by arousing your sympathy. They play the victim role which might be characterized like this...

Sigh. ..nothing I do seems to go right. Just look at the problems this assignment is causing me. I really appreciate you're giving me a hand to get things straight...

The <u>victim</u> is displaying the <u>upset</u> emotion that is coming from his, or her, child ego. Children cry for help and find comfort in other people doing things for them. It's their way of feeling wanted and comfortable when they find that they don't know what to do next . They usually want someone to tell them what to do because they have no success path of their own.

The Rescuer
Another game that people play, which is related to the game of "Victim" is the game of "Rescuer". This is the person who gets satisfaction out of helping people out...

"Here let me do that for you – just dump it on my desk!"
"Got a problem- just let me get down there and take a look at it".

This person has a need to be liked and can get it by taking other people's work and other people's problems onto his own shoulders. He isn't really helping the other person as they should be helping themselves. And this person is not focusing on his or her own problems. The "rescuer" is using the wrong means to feel O.K.

The Persecutor
A third kind of game is that of "Persecutor". The persecutor plays at bullying other people. Or continually planning to get his, or her own back on

someone. They are often deliberately obstructive to other people's success, whilst climbing on their backs to achieve personal success. The persecutor feels "O.K." about himself but that other people are not "O.K". he harbours grudges and was probably a bully in the school yard and practices the same methods for getting his own way in the workplace.

So when you recognize that someone is playing a game on you what do you do?

There are several other games that people play but "Victim" "Rescuer" and "Persecutor" are the three most common and easily recognizable. So what do you do?

You simply refuse to play!

Why? Because none of these games can ever have a positive "I win - You Win" outcome.

When someone is playing the victim, you do not play the rescuer.

When someone is playing the persecutor, you do not allow yourself to play victim.

You do not yourself play victim because you do not

need a rescuer.

You do not play <u>persecutor</u> because this would be over-assertive and will not produce an appropriate response.

Simply step aside. Use the rational, analytical thought- process of your adult ego to determine what's really going on. What is the real problem that needs your attention and what is really behind the behaviour that is confronting you?

When you do have a confrontational problem which is going to require your assertiveness, you should really take some time to plan a framework for the confrontation. Before you get on the intercom and call someone into your office take the time to plan the following four stages in the "negotiation" that you will be about to tackle

Getting someone to switch attitude does require negotiation and tact and not force and pressure.

1. What behaviour do you want to switch to what behaviour? What behaviour relates to what problem...what lies behind the problem? To get back to our earlier example Peter Brigg's constant lateness is the problem, but what is the behaviour, or

attitude behind the problem? Maybe Peter Brigg's negative behaviour stems from his unhappiness with the behaviour of one of his workmates. Is he perhaps behaving negatively because he is going through a divorce, or has some other domestic problem?

So how do you want him to behave? What do you consider appropriate?

2. Be prepared to explain precisely what negative effect this behaviour is having on you personally. Not on your company, or other workers, but you personally.

The reason for this is that assertiveness practises are geared around a personal one-on-one interaction. Tell the other person that you have a problem as a result of his or her behaviour. By changing their behaviour they will have helped you and will themselves benefit in some way.

It's most important that you plan not to lay blame on the other person, or use judgmental statements from your Parent Ego. It's a simple straight forward statement that his, or her, behaviour is causing a problem for you personally and you'd like to get to the bottom of the problem and, if possible, remove the problem. By laying blame for the problem, the other person will probably assume a defensive position, reducing the possibility of an "I Win - You Win" outcome.

3. Be prepared to give logical and rational reasons why the other person should change their behaviour. You will not inspire changes in behaviour if you don't get the other person to want to change.

People don't change because you want them to, they change because they want to change. That's something important to consider. People have to want to change of their own accord and the only way that can happen is if you supply them with logical, rational reasons why they should. These reasons are supplied through your Adult Ego.

4. The fourth thing that you'll need to plan before the confrontation, or negotiation, takes place is exactly what you're going to ask for.

It will be too late afterwards to think," Gee, I should have got some stronger kind of agreement over this. Now where do I stand?"

In nearly all cases, where problem-solving is your

requirement, you'll plan to ask commitment from the other party that some change will take place. "I'll try" is not an acceptable commitment. Why? It has a built-in failure mechanism. The other person, having failed to switch his behaviour, or change his attitude can just turn around and say *"I kept my promise didn't I? I said I'll try and I did".*

In important cases of problem solving it's often best to make an agreement on paper. One copy goes to the other party and the other copy goes into your business files. You and the other party both sign. Even on a simple matter such as absenteeism, after the behaviour has been discussed, the negative effect on yourself has been explained, logical rational reasons for making a change of behaviour have been supplied, then a simple agreement can be drawn up. It's amazing how two lines, neatly typed on a piece of paper can make a powerful agreement between two people. Whereas spoken promises are apt to be quickly forgotten, written words can be hauled out of the file at any time and used to face the other party, should the situation again occur

So if you are to be meeting with someone and your "confrontation" is going to be of a problem-solving nature remember to plan the four elements.

Plan first to talk about the behaviour, rather than the problem and know what behaviour you want switched for what.

Second explain the negative effect that it is having on you personally without laying blame on the other person (in any event they may be totally unaware that their behaviour is having a negative effect on you).

Thirdly give logical, rational reasons why the person should change. And fourthly, know in advance what commitment, verbal, or written you want from the other party.

Of course, not every situation requiring your assertiveness will be of a "problem-solving" nature. You can use assertiveness techniques to prevent problems. You can start talking to people early so that you can nip developing problems in the bud and avoid patterns developing.

Just call in the other person and ask "Is there a problem"? Listen to the other point of view and then attempt to engage in a mutually respectful exchange of information.

CHECKLISTS

To conclude this part of the book on Assertive Behaviour" let's run through a checklist of requirements for a truly assertive situation:

1. Begin by feeling OK about yourself. If you don't feel OK write out a block of cards and read the appropriate affirmations over and over to yourself.

2. Always try to make the other party feel OK even if it goes against the grain. You will not motivate compliance by being blameful and steam-rolling from your managerial position.

3. Beware of Judgmental words, or put downs like *"This is the kind of bad behaviour I've grown to expect from you! It's your fault that we're in this mess!"*

4. Use the words "I" and "Me" instead of the words "We" and "Us". I think that...not We think that. Always try to establish a one-on-one person communication. Talk more about what you need for yourself and how the other person will be helping you by complying with your wishes.

5. Invite responses from the other person. What do you feel about that? Can you suggest a way we can agree on that? What seems to be the problem? How do you see us going on from here?

6. Try to be open-minded at all times. Invite co-operation. Influence other people rather than force them to change.

7. Don't correct people's mistakes in front of others.

8. Don't play the games that people play, like the Victim, the Rescuer and the Persecutor. Someone in all of these games ends up feeling not OK.

9. Become a good listener. Listen creatively whilst the other person is talking.

10. Be mindful of body language... notice when you have lost good eye contact and the other person is fidgeting uncomfortably. Know when to change your ploy through observation of the other person's body language. And use good body language yourself. Use good eye contact without staring. Use nods of agreement. Sit in a relaxed manner. Use a friendly smile. Don't lose your composure. Don't point your fingers. Don't clench your fists and look up to heaven for help. Don't tense your jaw, or grit your teeth.

11. Diffuse all emotional situations. Use your adult ego for logical, rational, analytical thinking. If your own temperature has risen dangerously high, change the subject..or ask a question...or even get up and excuse yourself from the meeting on some pretext, or other. If the other person's emotional barometer is rising too high, use body language and verbal reassurance to bring down the temperature before carrying on. Use relaxed voice tones. No raised voices.

12. Don't ever use blameful, or threatening behaviour. Point out logical consequences of unacceptable behaviour. It's better to say "I need your co-operation on this one Jim, can we talk about the problem I have?" rather than "It's all your fault you lazy bum. Do that one more time and you're fired!"

13. Recognise the ego state from which the other person is behaving and address it appropriately with your adult ego.

14. Use assertiveness to prevent problems arising, or patterns of problems developing, by bringing possible problems quickly out into the open. People tend to save up emotions like trading stamps and then blow up and trade in the whole book in one go.

Use assertiveness to discourage this type of "stamp" collecting.

15. Use assertiveness techniques in all confrontational situations - or people problems. There are only two reasons for anyone not doing what you're asking them to do for you. That's <u>can't</u> and <u>won't</u>!

One they can't because they don't have the tools, or equipment, or education, or training, or physical, or mental ability. Two is that they <u>won't</u> because they don't see why they should, or they simply don't want to, for any of many personal reasons. If they have the tools to do the job, use rational, logical, analytical thought processes of your adult ego to persuade them that they do want to do that thing for you.

16. Refrain from making personal remarks and personal criticism, always bring the conversation back to the effect that the behaviour is having on you personally.

17. Always strive for that important "I win -You win" situation. It's the true foundation for success in all personal interactions and confrontations.

It's true that Leaders are born but only in the same way as you, or I were born. Leadership is an overall ability that comes from acquiring a number of skills, amongst them The Creative Thinking Skill, The skill of Delegation, the Skill of Managing Time, the Skills of Negotiating and Dealing with Problem People... the Skill of Creative Listening, the Skill of Communicating... and other skills.

The way in which you practise these skills can be highly motivational for those who work under you, with you and above you. When you can inspire motivation you will have followers. When you have followers you will be a Leader.

Part TWO

DELEGATION

Leaders have followers and a leader's position is upfront with a committed and motivated team behind. But how does one become an inspirational leader? What makes subordinates give you their commitment? Research has identified a number of skills which have helped managers achieve extraordinary results through the use of their subordinates.... skills which give them the Leader's Edge. Now we will examine one of the most important skills of all...the skill of DELEGATION. We will examine why you should delegate, when you should delegate - and when you shouldn't.

 We will discuss how to make effective **work** assignments, how to put in controls and how to get feedback. We will also examine the all-important interpersonal relationship   that must be developed between yourself and your subordinates...all of which will help give you that important "slight edge" over the rest of the executive field. I call it...the LEADER'S EDGE!

WHY DELEGATE?

Let's examine the subject of "delegation" beginning with the question - why do it? Well, there are four main reasons. The first being simply that you have too much to do, to do it all yourself!

Reason number 1
As a manager you're not responsible for turning out a countable number of anything in a day.

Your day isn't done when so many boxes have been stacked, or so many wires joined together. Management isn't quantifiable in that way. There are very few parameters in management that can keep the job down to a known and confined size. In fact the job of being a manager tends to swell with your responsibilities - and as new responsibilities crop up all the time, the job tends to get bigger and bigger until an interesting point is reached. That is, *when the responsibilities that you have begin to outstrip your human capacity for handling them.*

The moment arrives when you have the responsibility for doing things but there is no way enough time, physical energy, or attention that you can give to them yourself.

Now, you have accepted those responsibilities and not to act on them in some way means that you're not being an effective manager. A typical example of this is the owner-manager, the entrepreneur, who works with the lads all day on doing jobs, then takes home his "management" work in a briefcase for a second 10 hour session when he gets home.

This kind of manager gets about four hours rest a day and still doesn't discharge all of his responsibilities. Even after his wife and children have left him - which can and often does happen - he still can't get everything done.

In time he just burns up because of the management side of his life - the bit that he does at home - interferes with his ability to supervise correctly during the day. And vice-versa. And it certainly isn't only owner-managers of businesses who work themselves into the ground like this, many executives work like this, for reasons that we'll go into later.

So one very big reason for learning the fine art of

delegation is that your actual real responsibilities (and I don't mean those obvious time- wasting things that you know you could get rid of if you put your mind to it) but your actual real responsibilities, usually spread over a wider area than is within your capacity to handle.

There just isn't enough time and mental and physical resources within yourself to do everything in your working day that you'd like to do.

Reason number 2
The next important reason for learning to delegate is that you will invariably get better results through making more use of your people. You will have more motivated staff, who will give you more commitment and better performance in the long run.
Behavioral scientists tell us that of all the psychology invented to motivate employees and subordinates, there's nothing that works as well as "giving them assurances that you genuinely believe in them".

By delegating effectively to subordinates you are, in fact, recognising and acknowledging their capabilities.
 Employees who are given responsibility tend to flourish. By <u>not</u> delegating to them you are in fact implying *"you're too stupid for this work assignment.*

I'm doing it myself because I don't believe you can handle it". Now that's very demotivational. Maybe you <u>don't</u> think that they can do the job and you do have to do it yourself. Which brings us to the next important reason for delegating.

Reason number 3
The third reason for delegating is that delegation through the making of effective work assignments, becomes a training function. Leadership comes not so much out of trying to gain something but out of trying to contribute something. In training your people to stretch a little, learn a little more and confidently perform a little better, you are contributing to their personal improvement. You are at the same time winning yourself disciples. And never forget, the only way you can build leadership is to build followers. Without followers there are no leaders.

Reason number 4
The fourth important reason for delegating is to make yourself a more effective manager and leader. If you don't have to do all of the "doing" yourself, as well as all of the decision-making, supervising, controlling and development of people and situations, you end up with more free time to do bigger and better things.

We've so far discussed the four main reasons for delegating effectively. First, you reduce the area of personal responsibility for tasks so that it doesn't overlap your personal capacity for task handling.

Second, it's highly motivational for subordinates to have you work through them, rather than over them...in removing some of your workload they actually become better producers in themselves.

Thirdly delegation offers an excellent opportunity for on-the-job training, giving subordinates opportunity for self-advancement, which is also highly motivational and tends to bond the team with the leader.

Fourth effective delegation and decentralisation of decision-making frees your time to concentrate on your job of leading your team.

THE CONCEPT OF DELEGATION

Now let's talk about the <u>concept</u> of delegation. Choose from the following five suggestions what you think delegation ought to be.

1. Delegation is getting rid of everything that you don't want to do yourself.

2. Delegation is giving out everything that the staff knows how to do and doing the rest yourself.

3. Delegation is ordering people about.

4. Delegation is getting someone else to do some of your work.

5 Delegation is handing down responsibility

Which do you choose for a definition of delegation? Well if you chose number one, you'd be... incorrect. Getting rid of everything that you don't want to do yourself, has its appeal. But this is actually "dumping" your workload. Your subordinate feels dumped-on. He, or she, feels that they are doing "your" job and he's only getting paid for doing "their" job.

Giving out everything that the staff knows how to do - and doing the rest yourself isn't correct either.

That's because if a job comes along and no member of your staff knows how to do it, you're always going to end up doing it yourself. And subordinates are quick to cotton-on that anything they can't do, you're only too willing to take off their plates for them. For example *"I can't work out that diagram..! Think I'd better leave it for the boss. Can't show him that I can do it otherwise he'll be for ever dumping that kind of job on me!"*

Delegation is "ordering people about". We'll that's partly true. You do have to order people about in order to delegate.

But just ordering people about doesn't necessarily guarantee results does it?

Number 5 is the correct answer!
Number five is the answer as to what is really delegation. "Delegation" is...<u>the handing down of responsibility</u>. It means decentralising your decision-making by having responsible people, who are motivated to achieve goals and objectives, to make certain decisions and take certain actions on your behalf.

There are THREE attitudes to consider
Delegation is a "Management Technique" and like all other management techniques, it implies some kind of an <u>interpersonal relationship</u> between the manager, or leader, and his or her team of

subordinates. It's up to you to learn how to develop and conduct that relationship - and the way in which you go about this "interpersonal relationship" will determine your failure, or success, as a delegator and leader.

To begin there are <u>three</u> attitudes to consider.

1. How do you see yourself as a manager?

2. How do you see your subordinates in your working arena?

3. How do your subordinates see you in <u>their</u> workplace? These are the three attitudes that control the "interpersonal relationship".

How do you see yourself as a manager?
Let's examine how you see yourself as a manager, or supervisor. Answer these questions...

Are <u>you</u> the only one with enough drive, initiative, knowledge and hands-on experience to really get things done around your place? Are you the only one who cares to shoulder responsibility for decision-making? Are you the only one in your business, or your department, who has enough authority to take the ball and run with it when opportunity occurs?

Did you perhaps start the business yourself, doing just about everything there was to be done? Or perhaps did you come up the hard way having worked up from the factory floor, hands-on, along the way?

Do you still get involved hands-on from time to time, showing your subordinates how you'd like the job done best?

If you answer "yes" to most of these questions, or even some of them, it means that you probably spend a large part of your day <u>doing</u> jobs yourself. You might even be the *"superdoer"* we described earlier, the person who spends the whole day doing jobs and in addition spends a couple of hours before the office opens and a lot more after it's closed, on management functions.

If this is indeed honestly how you see yourself, in whole, or even in part, you cannot be a good <u>delegator</u> without changing your attitude. You can't be a "doer" and a manager. A manager's job is to manage that things get done through other people, not to actually do things himself, or herself. It's the "doer's" job to do things and the manager's job to manage that the doers get the job done right.

Many smaller businesses, and entire departments within larger businesses, go on year after year making reasonable achievement and profit for the shareholders. Then they seem to reach a certain level of development and don't seem to go much further. The reason for this is often that the people in charge, the owners, the managers, the department heads, simply refuse to hand down responsibility. They insist on achieving results personally and do not believe that they can achieve, or know how to achieve, results thorough other people. Many small businesses actually fail because, in effect, the owner-manager hires people to sit around and watch him work.

Bigger businesses might not fail but an examination will usually reveal departments where the manager's problem of being a compulsive "doer" is a serious handicap on the development of the entire department. And this mind-set will never, ever, allow the manager to move on to leadership.
The "interpersonal relationship" mentioned earlier depends heavily on the leader-manager seeing himself as just that. His role in business life is to plan, to organise, to control, to direct, to communicate with and develop those who work under him into a motivated enthusiastic team of people through whom

he can get jobs done right... and <u>this</u> is how you should see <u>yourself</u>.

How do you see the team?
The next of the three <u>attitudes</u> to examine is how you see the team. Those subordinates who work under you, are they in fact a team? Or do you see them as a bunch of order takers...people who do exactly what you tell them and report back when they've finished, so that they can pick up the next work assignment?

Do you worry about giving them responsibility because you know that it's against human nature for subordinates to accept responsibility. Do you <u>know</u> that there will be a foul-up if you give them jobs to do that might be a little ahead of what they're used to doing?

Do you often think that by the time you've trained up someone to do a particular task, you could have done it yourself in half the time? Do you like to be informed step-by-step on the progress of work you've given out and then, if trouble arises, do you feel the need to take over the reins yourself? Do you have people working for you who are doing more or less the same jobs that they were doing a couple of years ago? People who just haven't advanced?

If this is roughly how you see <u>your subordinates</u> you are again going to need to make an attitude shift before you can become a respected delegator. If you see your subordinates like this, they will behave as you see them. If you're always going to save the day if something goes wrong, why should <u>they</u> worry about the job? If you are always going to carry the can for whatever happens, why should they care about responsibility? If they see <u>nothing</u> at which they have an opportunity to excel then they have no opportunity for achievement and will therefore earn no recognition, or advancement within the company.

You can't successfully delegate to people who are of this frame of mind. Remember part of your role as a manager-leader is to communicate with and develop your people. This is how your subordinates like to see you. This is the correct attitude for motivated response from your subordinates.

How do your subordinates see you?
The third point about attitude is to be aware of how your employees, subordinates, or team members, see you. Do they already see you as their leader? Do they see you as their manager? Do they see you as "the boss"? The person who doles out the work assignments and who kicks their butts when they don't perform? And why is it important how

they see you? It's important because of the interpersonal relationship that must be developed.

It works on the basis of give and take and mutual respect by the manager of the subordinate and by the subordinate of the manager.

Answer the following questions and see how well you are respected by your subordinates...

1) Do you start people working on one job and then often pull them off onto another?
2) Do you prefer to do the difficult bit yourself?
3) Do you expect absolute perfection?
4) Do you roast failures over the coals?
5) Do you usually delegate only short-term work assignments and build in constant checks?
6) Do you reserve absolute authority and decision-making for yourself?
7) Do you firmly believe that none of your subordinates can do the job as well as you can do it?
8) Do you have a general lack of confidence in your subordinates?
9) Do you feel that you have no-one to delegate to?
10) Do you like to modify the work assignment as the job progresses, rather than map out a complete assignment right at the beginning?
11) Do you expect all things to be done your way?

If the answer to these questions is generally "YES", you don't shape up too well as a good boss let alone as a respected leader of motivated staff. Not in your subordinate's eyes anyway.

If you do these things you are not only going to make a poor delegator but those to whom you wish to delegate will be largely unreceptive. The mutual respect that tends to get things done quicker and better and more creatively, won't be there. Let's see why not, using the questions you've just answered as examples.

If you tend to pull your people off one job and put them onto another, unless it's unavoidable, you will be seen by your subordinates as an indecisive manager. Someone who can't make up their mind. And that's hardly a leadership quality!

Saving the most difficult bit for yourself to do implies that you don't trust your subordinates to do the job for you. They will see you as putting them down, stifling their ability to succeed at something.

If you insist on absolute perfection from your subordinates you are probably unnecessarily fussy and ruffling a lot of feathers along the way. Most times an <u>acceptable</u> standard that is cost-effective to produce, is good enough.

If you berate your subordinates for their failures, calling them "stupid" "lazy" "good-for-nothings", they're hardly going to want to accept responsibility for the job next time round, now are they? You alienate them with this kind of behaviour.

Short-term work assignments with an overdose of checking and controls built-in, again demonstrates that you have no faith in your subordinate's ability to succeed with any major, or substantial task. If you don't believe in them, do you have a right to expect them to believe in you?

If you reserve absolute authority and decision-making for yourself, you are not handing down responsibility and are failing at delegation. Subordinates respect good delegators because a well delegated work assignment lets a subordinate know exactly what you want done, how and when you want it done, and to what standards. A poorly delegated work assignment leaves a subordinate wondering what he's really supposed to be doing and feeling that he might get the blame later for you not having set out the job clearly.

If you believe that nobody else can do the job as well as you , it's probably because you have not <u>trained</u> anyone else to do the that job as well as you can. The same goes for the feeling that there is no-one you can delegate to and the general lack of confidence in subordinates. Training your people to accomplish tasks and setting up controls to check that these tasks are properly accomplished is the basis of good delegation. Subordinates respect being trained to do something. Those companies that have bright, efficient, motivated staff, aren't just the lucky ones who scooped all of the good guys out of the employment agency. They are the companies that trained and developed their people.

If you like to get people started on a project, work their way into it and model the work assignment as the job goes along, then you are not setting clear objectives for the assignment...which is highly frustrating for those working on the task because they don't know where, how, or even "if" it will end.

And do you like everything done <u>your</u> way? Well, if so it's fairly natural for a manager to think like that because doing things your way was good enough to get you the manager's job in the first place. But you must realise that some people like to do things different ways and you have to give them some leeway. The important thing is nearly always the end result, not necessarily how that result was achieved. So to get the respect of your subordinates you, as a manager, must cut them some slack to do the job the way <u>they</u> see it should be done.

SUMMARY - ATTITUDES

So much for the <u>interpersonal relationship</u>. Just to recap briefly, we talked about the <u>three attitudes,</u> which are; How do you see yourself as a manager? How do you see your subordinates, or emoployees, in their workplace? and How do your subordinates, or your team, see you as their manager, or leader? These attitudes when fine-tuned and in concert with each other form the ideal background for good delegation. If your attitude is one of a "doer" and not manager, you can't effectively delegate and you cannot become a leader. If you don't see your subordinates as trustworthy beings who must be trained up to accept responsibility, you also can't delegate effectively.

And you can't delegate effectively if your subordinates don't respect you as someone who is going to use them effectively and sympathetically to get results. You'll see from all of this that "delegation" is very much a management skill. When effective, it also contributes greatly to the motivation and commitment that you'll need from followers, if you want to become a leader.

Two vital principles
Two vital principles of delegation are
1) training and 2) Control.

You cannot hand down responsibility to any old body and then kick his butt if the job doesn't get done right. You shouldn't drop your subordinates in at the deep end and see if they sink, or swim. You have to train your subordinates on an ongoing basis to achieve your objectives, in line with overall company objectives, so that you can be pretty sure that a subordinate is capable of performing the work assignment that you give to him, or her.

Then you have to input some kind of control so that you know that the job is being done to the standard you've prescribed. The control is just as important as the training because if you don't have accurate feedback you can't be sure that the job is done properly and you get back to square one of not trusting your subordinate to do it, so you'd better do it yourself.

It's also important to remember that you might be giving out a work assignment to someone who's never done such a job before.

Although you're perfectly familiar with how to do it and would , of course, get it right first time, they might struggle.

Give them a little help and a little patience. Excellence, remember, comes from the experience of doing things right. Experience in the first place comes from doing things wrong!

So the second point I've made regarding <u>attitude</u> is that you must have the inclination to train and develop your people to <u>accept delegation from you.</u> That is, the responsibilities that you'll be handing down.

Your subordinates must be given responsibility for things like planning, scheduling, keeping materials flowing, dealing with workers at production level. They must be acknowledged for their successes and rewarded in some way for their achievements (and here I don't necessarily mean financial rewards).

Your subordinates should also be expected to carry responsibility for their failures - although the ultimate responsibility for failure would rest on you. All of these things amount to greater job satisfaction and nearly always, greater motivation for the subordinate.

SOME PRACTICAL 'HOW-TO'S"

Next I will bring you some more positive "How To" kind of information. Later in this book we'll discuss how to actually make an effective work assignment, How to remove the road blocks to effective delegation, how to delegate the work assignment and reasons still for failure to delegate.
 I will also try to answer outstanding questions that you might have about delegation in your particular circumstance.

So how do we make an effective work assignment?

To illustrate a point would you call in your engineer and say, *"Bill I want you to erect a suspension bridge over here on the map, get on with it will you?* Of course you wouldn't, because Bill would need to have plans, schedules, details, costings, timing, geological surveys, surveys of quantities, labour details and a host of other information. And you would need to have inspectors and a whole lot of controls to make sure that the job was on schedule and to the approved standard.   That seems obvious but there are many managers who might say to their subordinate, *"Harry, the new injection-moulding machine has just arrived, please see that it's installed will you?*

 Now this is a relatively simple work assignment - and for this reason it was thoughtlessly delegated. And it quite often is the smaller jobs that gum up the works because they are badly delegated.

Harry would definitely be unhappy with such an assignment which was badly made for three reasons.

1. You didn't explain the job.

2. You didn't get a commitment from Harry that he could, or would do it.

3. You didn't explain to Harry what the follow-up, or control, was going to be to check that the job was done right

With this kind of delegation Harry would not be a happy "follower" and your standing as a leader would be diminished.

The above three points form the basis of a good work

assignment. First you explain the job. Second, you get commitment. And third you incorporate a follow-up procedure.
Let's examine these points one at a time.

Defining the Job
What is it exactly that has to be done? Take the time and trouble to explain this. What are the priorities? What should be tackled first, second, third? Now you must say what standards of performance you expect. That is what quality you expect, what quantity you expect and in what time frame you expect the job to be finished.(In other words, what are you criteria for acceptance that the end result is up to your expectations?)

Also, you must explain at what point you will consider that the job has been successfully completed. For example, is Harry's part of the job completed when the machine is off the truck and bolted down against the factory wall? Or is the assignment completed when the machine is wired up, powered up and ready to run? Or is the assignment completed when a seven-hour test run has been made of the equipment in full operation?

Whilst explaining the job you must also explain what authority your subordinates will have during the assignment and what responsibility they will have. This is a very important part of defining the assignment. How many times has a subordinate come to you and said *"It wasn't my fault it went wrong, it wasn't my job to check so-and-so"?*

Getting commitment
You have explained the job to your subordinate. You now have to get their commitment to achieving the results that you expect.

You do this by first discussing the project with your subordinate, all of the time focusing your discussion upon the results that you expect. Solicit ideas from your subordinate on how they feel that the job should be done. Don't do all of the talking. Become a good listener. Get your subordinates to agree that they will take responsibility for the assignment the way you have laid it out and also that your expectations are *reasonable* and *attainable.*

At this point you should also offer your assistance, that is in your role as a manager, should anything begin to go wrong. This does not mean that you should be called immediately every time a minor decision has to be made. And it certainly doesn't mean that you'll come on over and pick up the job from where it went wrong. It means rather that you are offering support as a leader. Remember that managers are there to manage the "doer" not to do those things themselves.

Still under the heading of "Getting Commitment", you should also discuss at what point the progress of the work should be checked and against what standards it will be checked. If you agree at this point with your subordinates on the check-point procedure, they won't feel that you are looking over their shoulder later and keeping tabs on them because you don't really trust them to do the work.

The follow-up or Control

The third part of making an effective work assignment is the follow-up or control. You must review the work assignment periodically as pre-arranged with your subordinate. Check on what difficulties have arisen and how they have been dealt with. If difficulties are persisting offer your assistance, again as a manager and not as a "doer" to sort out the problem.

Assess the progress of the job according to pre-agreed standards. If the job is going to take three months, check your indicators once a month to see that all is well. Remember, your subordinate gave you a commitment to certain standards when you explained the job to him and you now have to assess that those pre-arranged standards are being met. If they are not being met, get a report-back on why not. And that report should be factual and specific and not personal and full of excuses and alibis. If necessary you should remind your subordinate of the responsibility that they accepted – which is equally a responsibility for failure as for success. However, you should also recognize that unforeseen problems do sometimes arise and that things can and do go wrong.

Don't change the work assignment along the way!
If at all possible do not make changes once the work has started. If you do need to make significant changes then the work assignment should be re-presented in a modified form. Once more you should go through the three stages of making a work assignment
1. By re-defining the modified task
2. Once more getting the subordinate's commitment to the modified task
3. By re-agreeing to the control and follow-up.

DELEGATING THE WORK ASSIGNMENT

Making an effective work assignment is one thing. Handing out responsibility for it is something else.

Many managers do make effective work assignments but they still experience difficulty in actually delegating. This could be for a number of reasons which need explaining. I call them "The Barriers to Effective Delegation".

Most of the "barriers" stem from the manager having been at one time, used to doing the job himself. He, or she, has never quite shed the feeling of being a "doer". Yet they can't afford to be a "doer" any more in their career as a manager-leader. Top executives cannot afford to spend more than one or two per cent of their time being a "doer". First line managers who work directly at the coal face with the people who are "doers" may find themselves forced into hands-on "doing" for about thirty per cent of their time.

Always remember that being a great "doer" in management will never make you a great leader. So take note of the following barriers to effective delegation and cross over them wherever and whenever you can!

1. The first barrier is that you may simply like to do things yourself.
Doing things that you're good at is often a lot more fun and can be more satisfying than managing others to do those things. So there's a tendency to take

things out of the hands of your subordinates and to do them yourself. If you are prone to this behavior you will find yourself doing more and more and your subordinates less and less. They don't mind at all standing back and watching you sweat, if that's the way you want to do it.

2. The second barrier is that you don't know what to delegate!
Delegation isn't getting someone else to do your work. If you consider yourself a manager then the choice is clear. You must delegate all "doing" work and free yourself for all matters to do with planning, organising, controlling, motivating and developin your subordinates.

3.The third barrier is lack of trust and confidence in your subordinates!
You must train up your people so that you can have confidence in them. Remove your mental bias that they might be too young, too old, too experienced, too foreign or the wrong sex to do the job. If a person hasn't tried a work-assignment before, who are you to say they can't do it? A subordinate who feels trusted to do the job becomes a motivated follower of their manager/leader .

4. The fourth barrier is the thought that you have no

time to delegate!
Training takes time. Making work assignments takes time. Why not just get in there and do the job yourself? Simply because you'll never get up the ladder if you are always standing on the bottom rung! You have to train people up so you can go up yourself.

5. A fifth barrier is fears and self-doubt!
Peope relatively new to management tend to experience a number of fears and concerns. They worry about their lack of tried and proven management skills and their inadequacies as new managers. A new manager who has been promoted from a "doer" to a manager will fear rejection by his or her workmates who are still "doers". GTis person tends to dabble around at doing things himself because he is embarrassed to delegate – personalities get in the way.

Or they may fear that their superiors do not see them working – because much of management's function cannot be seen, or easily measured, so he or she reverts to the "doing" jobs so that they can be seen to be working hard at something with measurable results.

Another fear is that training up subordinates, or handing over responsibility will put the manager's own job in danger. If the subordinate ends up doing the job as well as the manager did it before he became a manager, won't he end up with the manager's job some day?

The answer to this is that the manager must progress up the ladder and he or she should be training subordinates to fill their shoes. If you don't have somebody reliable under you to step into your position it's going to hamper your own upward career path. Help that subordinate to become a follower and you are helping yourself to become a leader.

6. A sixth barrier is a desire to be part of the action!
To sit down and manager requires a good deal of **mental discipline. To stand up and get stuck into the** task is much easier. A manager who is stuck on a mental problem, or may just not have much to do at the time will tend to go down to the work area and see how the lads are doing on the job he or she has set them. They will then pick on something that isn't being done quite the way they used to do it and they'll butt in and involve themselves in the assignment.

This, of course, alienates the subordinates who feel mistrusted and put down and it results in less effectiveness in the long run.

ACTIVITIES THAT CAN MAKE YOU A GOOD DELEGATOR

Try at all times to accomplish that vital shift from "doer" to manager. Delegate <u>everything</u> that is not a management function. The prime management functions are: to plan, organise, control, to direct, to motivate, communicate and develop your subordinates.

Learn *how* to train and develop your subordinates. Encourage them to admit their mistakes and to accept constructive criticism. Reassure them that you're not going to bite their heads off if they make a mistake. Teach them to accept you as playin g a supportive role.

Give out enough *authority* to your subordinates so that they can carry out the assignment efficiently without constantly referring back to you.

Give your people acceptable promotional opportunities. They must be able to advance themselves if they are to remain motivated. Be open to *their ideas on how the job should be done.*

Give credit where it's due. Don't steal your subordinate's achievement by claiming it for yourself as department head. A little recognition goes a long way.

Don't insist on absolute perfection at all times when there are times when an acceptable standard is all that's required in the end product.

Don't expect everything to be done your way. Allow some tolerance for others to do it their way. You may even have to accept that *their* way is better than *your* way. (If this is the case praise them, don't get all mean and twisted about it!)

Learn to part with some of your responsibility. Reward your subordinates for their successes but also make them accountable for their failures.

Don't make it personal when someone doesn't achieve for you. Don't berate people personally. Rather get to the bottom of the problem by looking at the facts.

Know what it is that you want done. Make up your mind fully before you make out the work assignment.

Set clear objectives, policies and guidelines when defining the work assignments and try not to change you mind during the course of the work assignment.

Make sure that the person to who you are delegating understands what is required. In fact make sure that you both understand each other.

Set priorities for your people so that they clearly understand what is most important and what they must tackle first, particularly if they are very busy at the time.

Learn to delegate the whole job and not just bits and pieces of it. Make your subordinates accountable for the entire project, where possible, and not just bits and pieces of it. This way they cannot turn around later and say that it was the bit someone else was handling that fouled up the bit that they were doing.

Always get feedback and control. You can't just hand over important tasks and expect them to be done. Establish a system of reporting from your subordinates so they know what's going on and if something is going wrong what corrective action can be taken before things get worse.

Always remember that your job as a manager is to get results through people. So you have to work *with* people, establishing a chain of command. And you must see that your chain of command doesn't get broken by somebody busting in from the top, possibly your own superior, who should not be delegating to your people without going through you.

CONCLUSION

I have introduced you to the concept of an interpersonal relationship necessary for effective delegation. I have outlined how a work assignment should be made out by first explaining the job, then getting commitment, then incorporating feedback and control procedures. Then I explained how the work assignment should be delegated and I revealed some of the barriers that block good delegation even after acceptable work assignments have been made out.

Grasp the principles and techniques outlined here and you'll find that you'll get much more out of your day. You will achieve more success, gain more recognition for your achievements.

Above all you will be a more effective manager, one with motivated followers, which means that you have gained "The Leader's-Edge". Thank you for reading my book.

Phil Sinclair

Note from the Publishers:

The skills of Assertive Behaviour and Delegation are two of the most vital of executive skills but they are not stand-alone-skills. These skills often interrelate with others, such as Time Management, Creative Thinking and Problem Solving, Negotiation, Team Building and others. The effective manager needs all of these skills in their tool kit and he/she needs a fast and dependable method of acquiring these skills.

Please visit our On-line shop where you can purchase self-development books, Cd's and downloads on personal skills development subjects for managers and aspiring leaders.

www.leadersedge.co.za

Printed in Great Britain
by Amazon.co.uk, Ltd.,
Marston Gate.